SYMBOLS & LINES

- - - - - - - - -
valley fold

— · — · — · —
mountain fold

++++++++++++++
Cut line

Turn over
or rotate

Fold then unfold

Pleat fold
(repeated
folding)

Crease line

SQUARING OFF PAPER

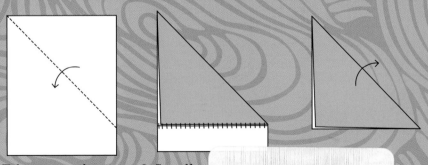

1. Take rectangular
sheet, valley fold
diagonally.

2. Cut off ex   square.
side as sh

BASIC FOLDS

KITE FORM

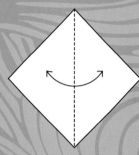 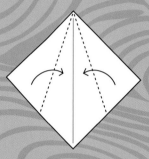 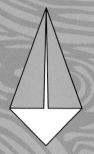

1. Fold and unfold a square diagonally, making a center crease.

2. Fold both sides in to the center crease.

3. This is a kite form.

VALLEY FOLD

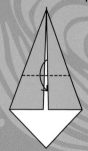

1. Here, using the kite, fold form toward you (forward), making a "valley."

2. This fold forward is a valley fold.

MOUNTAIN FOLD

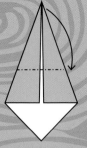

1. Here, using the kite, fold form away from you (backward), making a "mountain."

2. This fold backward is a mountain fold.

INSIDE REVERSE FOLD

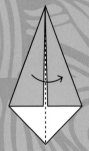

1. Here, using the kite, valley fold closed.

2. Valley fold as marked to crease, then unfold.

3. Pull tip in direction of arrow.

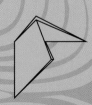

4. Appearance before completion.

5. You've made an inside reverse fold.

OUTSIDE REVERSE FOLD

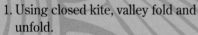

1. Using closed kite, valley fold and
   unfold.

2. Fold inside out, as shown by arrows.

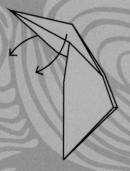

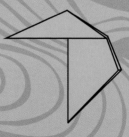

3. Appearance before completion.

4. You've made an outside reverse fold.

PLEAT FOLD

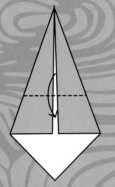 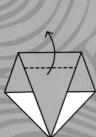 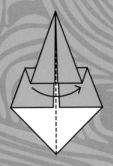 

1. Here, using the kite, valley fold.

2. Valley fold back again.

3. This is a pleat. Valley fold in half.

4. You've made a pleat fold.

PLEAT FOLD REVERSE

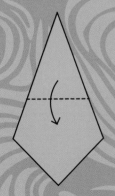 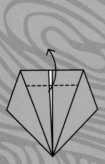 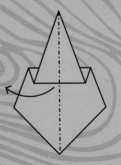 

1. Here, using the kite form backward, valley fold.

2. Valley fold back again for pleat.

3. Mountain fold form in half.

4. You've made a pleat fold reverse.

SQUASH
FOLD I

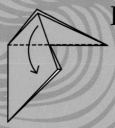 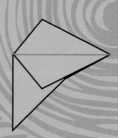

1. Using inside reverse, valley fold one side.

2. You've made a squash fold I.

SQUASH
FOLD II

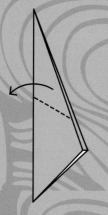  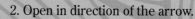

1. Using closed kite form, valley fold.

2. Open in direction of the arrow.

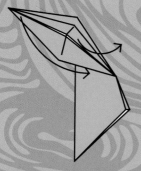 

3. Appearance before completion.

4. You've made a squash fold II.

INSIDE CRIMP FOLD

1. Here using closed kite form, pleat fold.

2. Pull tip in direction of the arrow.

3. You've made an inside crimp fold.

OUTSIDE CRIMP FOLD

  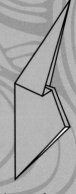

1. Here using closed kite form, pleat fold and unfold.

2. Fold mountain and valley as shown, both sides.

3. You've made an outside crimp fold.

BASE FOLDS

Base folds are basic forms that do not in themselves produce origami, but serve as a basis, or jumping-off point, for a number of creative origami figures—some quite complex. As when beginning other crafts, learning to fold these base folds is not the most exciting part of origami. They are, however, easy to do, and will help you with your technique. They also quickly become rote, so much so that you can do many using different-colored papers while you are watching television or your mind is elsewhere. With completed base folds handy, if you want to quickly work up a form or are suddenly inspired with an idea for an original, unique figure, you can select an appropriate base fold and swiftly bring a new creation to life.

BASE FOLD I

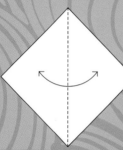

1. Fold and unfold in direction of arrow.

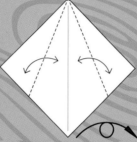

2. Fold both sides in to center crease, then unfold. Rotate.

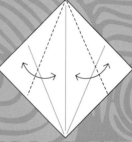

3. Fold both sides in to center crease, then unfold.

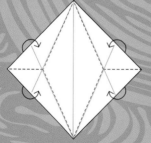

4. Pinch corners of square together and fold inward.

5. Completed Base Fold I.

BASE FOLD II

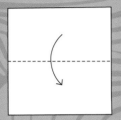

1. Valley fold.

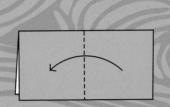

2. Valley fold.

3. Squash fold.

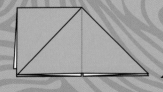

4. Turn over to other side.

5. Squash fold.

6. Completed Base Fold II.

BASE FOLD III

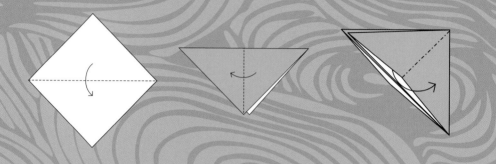

1. Valley fold.

2. Valley fold.

3. Squash fold.

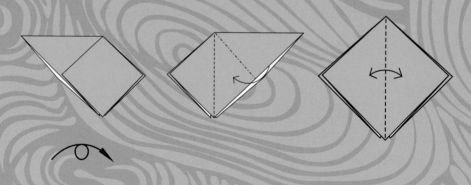

4. Turn over.

5. Squash fold.

6. Valley fold, then unfold.

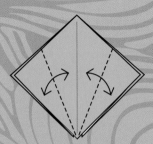

7. Make valley folds,
   then unfold.

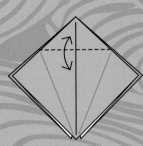

8. Valley fold, then
   unfold.

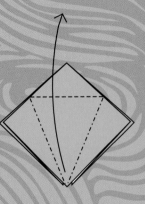

9. Pull in direction of
   arrow, folding inward
   at sides.

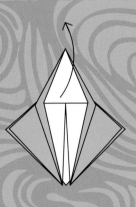

10. Appearance before
    completion of fold.

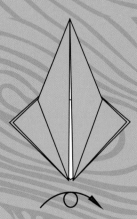

11. Fold completed.
    Turn over.

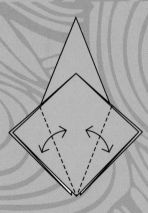

I2. Make valley folds,
    then unfold.

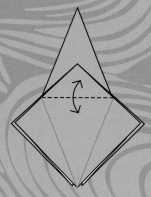

13. Valley fold, then unfold.

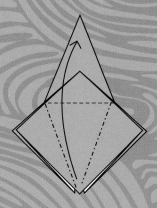

14. Repeat, again pulling in direction of arrow.

15. Appearance before completion.

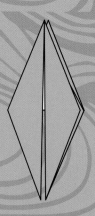

16. Completed Base Fold III.

BASE FOLD IV

1. Valley fold paper in half, and cut in half along middle crease. Valley fold in half as shown.

2. Valley fold in direction of arrow.

3. Make cut as shown.

4. Unfold.

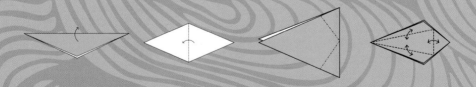

5. Unfold.

6. Valley fold in half.

7. Inside reverse fold to inner center crease.

8. Valley fold and unfold to crease.

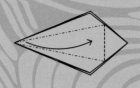 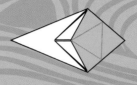 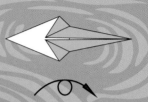

9. Pull in direction of arrow, and fold.

10. Appearance before completion.

11. Turn over.

12. Valley fold, then unfold.

13. Again, pull in direction of arrow, and fold.

14. Completed Base Fold IV.

STINGRAY

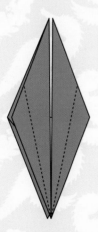

1. Start with Base Fold III. Make valley folds.

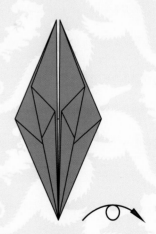

2. Turn over.

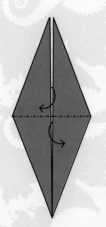

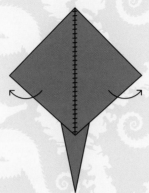

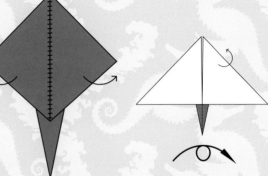

3. Squash fold.

4. Cut as shown, then make valley folds.

5. Mountain fold in half, then rotate into position of next step.

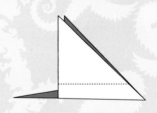

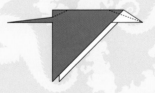

6. Valley fold both front and back.

7. Make valley folds to both sides.

8. Valley fold both front and back.

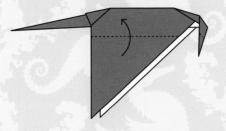

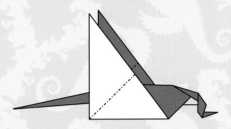

9. Make valley and mountain folds.

10. Mountain fold both sides. Apply glue to center of form.

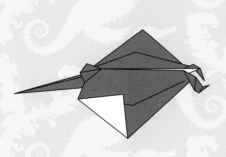

11. Completed Stingray.

HORSESHOE CRAB

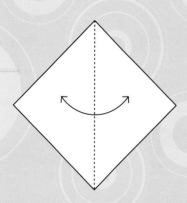

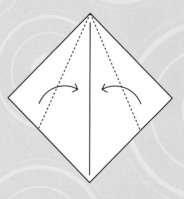

1. Start with a square piece of paper.
   Valley fold and unfold.

2. Fold both sides inward.

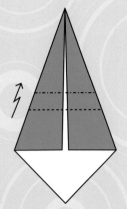

3. Pleat fold.

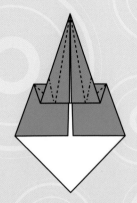

4. Make squash folds.

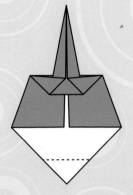

5. Valley fold.

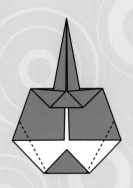

6. Make valley folds.

7. Make valley folds.

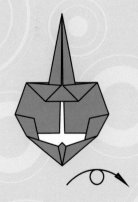

8. Turn over.

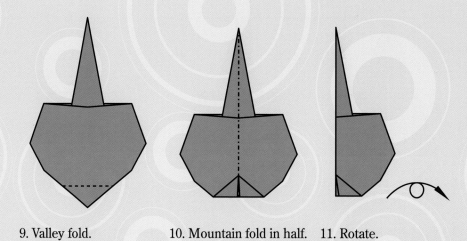

9. Valley fold.

10. Mountain fold in half.

11. Rotate.

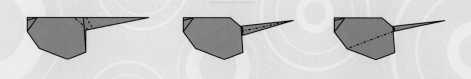

12. Crimp fold.

13. Mountain fold both sides.

14. Valley fold and unfold.

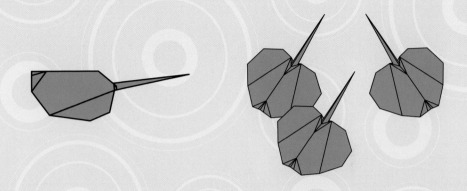

15. Unfold to flatten.

16. Completed Horseshoe Crab.

DOLPHIN

PART I

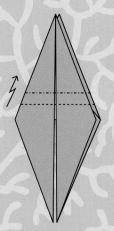

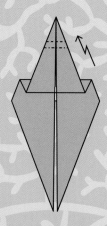

1. Start with Base Fold III. Pleat fold through all layers.

2. Repeat pleat fold through layers.

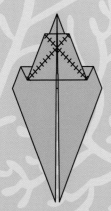

3. Make cuts as shown
   (to top layer only).

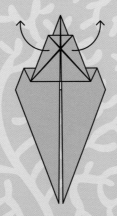

4. Make valley folds.

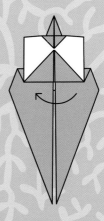

5. Valley fold in half.

6. Pull and crimp fold.

7. Pull and crimp fold.

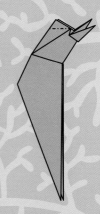

8. Mountain fold.

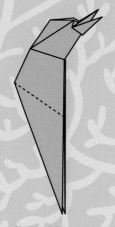

9. Make valley folds.

10. Mountain fold both sides.

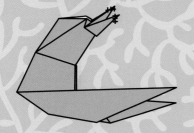

11. Make cuts as shown.

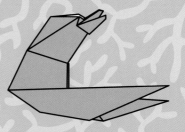

12. Completed part I of Dolphin.

PART II

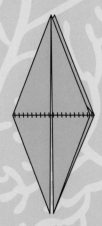

1. Start with Base Fold III. Cut as shown.

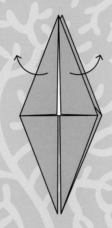

2. Make valley folds.

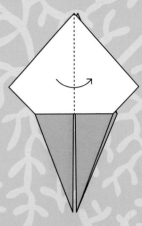

3. Valley fold in half.

4. Outside reverse fold.

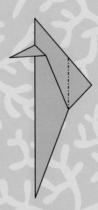

5. Mountain fold.

6. Pull paper outward at top; mountain fold below.

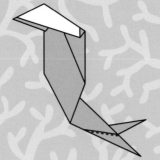

7. Outside reverse fold at top. Mountain fold below.

8. Valley fold and glue into position.

9. Completed part II of Dolphin.

TO ATTACH

1. Join parts together as shown.

2. Valley fold both sides.

3. Completed Dolphin.

CORAL FISH

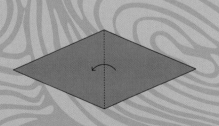

1. Valley fold in half.

2. Make inside reverse folds.

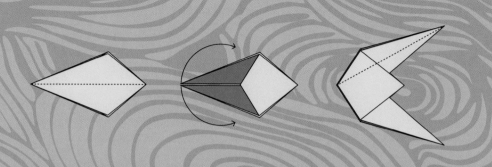

3. Valley fold both front and back.

4. Make inside reverse folds.

5. Valley fold both sides.

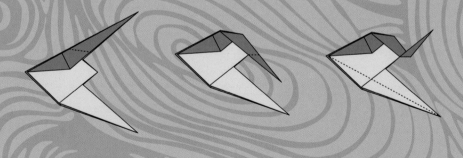

6. Outside reverse fold.

7. Outside reverse fold.

8. Valley fold both sides.

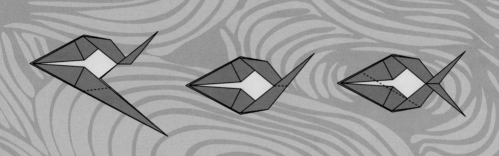

9. Outside reverse fold.   10. Outside reverse fold.   11. Valley fold layer to front.

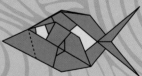

12. Valley fold.   13. Mountain fold to inside.   14. Valley fold.

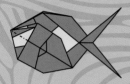

15. Mountain fold to inside.

16. Mountain fold to back.

17. Make cuts and valley fold out to sides both front and back.

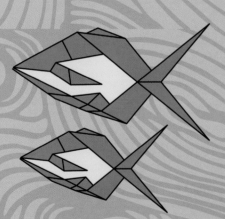

18. Completed Coral Fish.

ANGELFISH

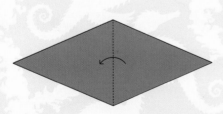

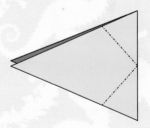

1. Start with step 5 (diamond shape) of Base Fold IV. Valley fold in half.

2. Make inside reverse folds.

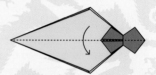

3. Make cuts to front layer only.

4. Valley fold cut parts.

5. Valley fold front and back.

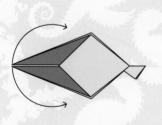

6. Make inside reverse folds.

7. Valley fold front and back.

8. Mountain fold layer inward.

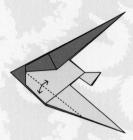

9. Valley fold layer and unfold.

10. Cut along crease. Valley fold.

11. Turn over to other side.

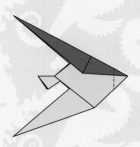

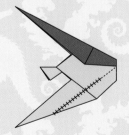

12. Mountain fold.

13. Cut as shown, then valley fold.

14. Valley fold both side fins outward.

15. Turn over.

16. Add color.

17. Completed Angelfish.

LIONFISH

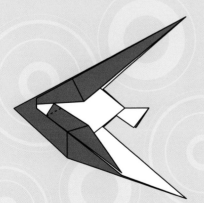

1. Start with step 11 of Angelfish
   (page 37). Valley fold.

12. Valley fold.

13. Valley fold.

14. Cut as shown.

15. Turn to the other side.

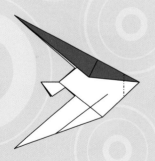

16. Mountain fold and glue to hold.

17. Valley fold.

18. Valley fold.

19. Valley fold.

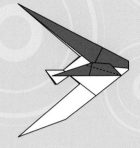

20. Valley fold.

21. Cut top layer as shown.

22. Valley unfold both front and back.

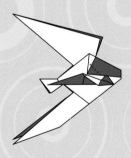

23. Valley fold both sides.

24. Make valley folds front and back.

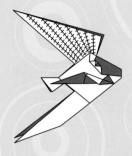

25. Make cuts as shown to both sides.

26. Repeat cuts to lower section.

27. Valley fold front and back.

28. Valley fold front and back.

29. Valley fold front and back.

30. Valley fold front and back.

31. Valley fold front and back.

32. Valley fold side fins loosely to extend.

33. Loosely valley fold at top, on both sides. Add any color and patterning wanted.

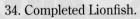

34. Completed Lionfish.

HAMMERHEAD SHARK

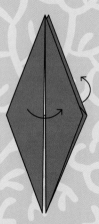

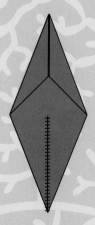

1 Start with Base Fold III. Valley fold one flap and repeat behind.

2. Cut as shown front and back.

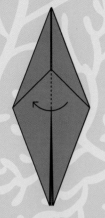

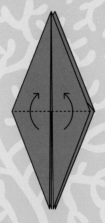

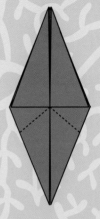

3. Valley fold flap back again. Repeat behind.

4. Make valley folds upward.

5. Make valley folds.

6. Turn over to the other side.

7. Valley fold.

8. Turn over to the other side.

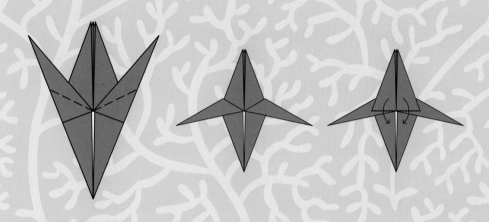

9. Make valley folds.   10. Pull inner layer out.   11. Make valley folds.

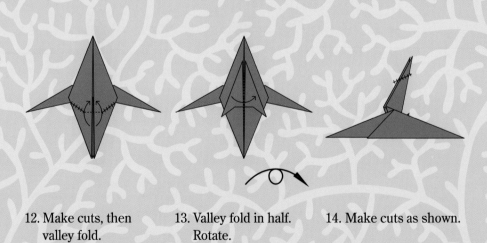

12. Make cuts, then
    valley fold.

13. Valley fold in half.
    Rotate.

14. Make cuts as shown.

15. Make valley folds
    both front and back.

16. Outside reverse fold.
    Valley fold.

17. Cut edge as shown.

18. Valley fold both front
    and back.

19. Squash fold both
    front and back.

20. Valley fold sides
    outward to balance.

21. Make cut as shown.

22. Make valley folds both front and back.

23. Make valley folds both front and back.

24. Make valley folds both front and back.

25. Mountain fold.

26. Make valley fold both sides and position to balance.

27. Adjust tail, fins, and head to balance.

28. Completed Hammerhead Shark.

SEAHORSE

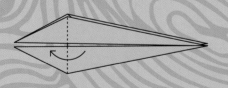

1. Start with Base Fold IV. Valley fold.

2. Turn over to other side.

3. Valley fold both sides.　　4. Inside reverse fold.　　5. Turn over to other side.

6. Make valley folds and squash folds.　　7. Rotate.　　8. Mountain fold in half.

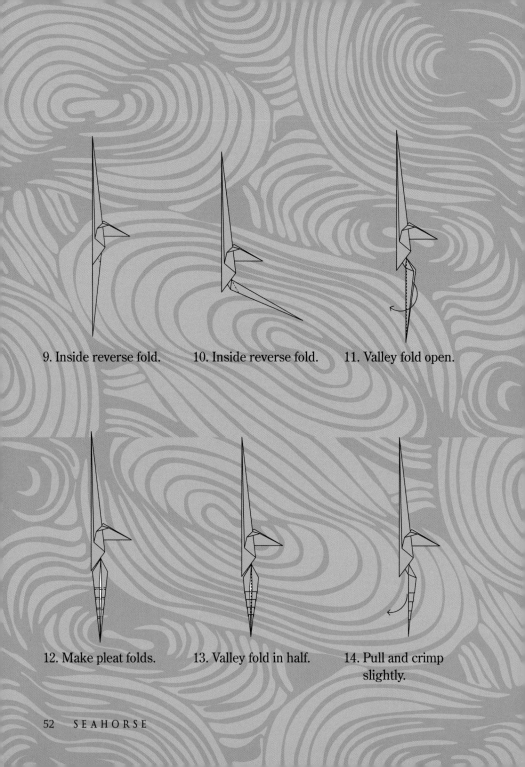

9. Inside reverse fold.

10. Inside reverse fold.

11. Valley fold open.

12. Make pleat folds.

13. Valley fold in half.

14. Pull and crimp slightly.

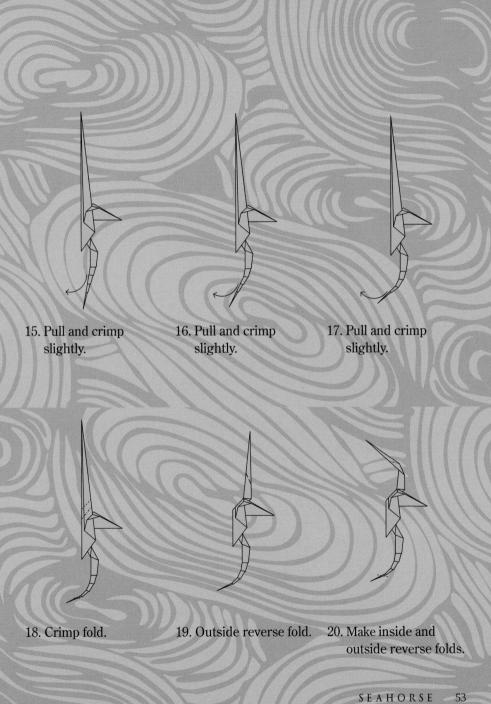

15. Pull and crimp slightly.

16. Pull and crimp slightly.

17. Pull and crimp slightly.

18. Crimp fold.

19. Outside reverse fold.

20. Make inside and outside reverse folds.

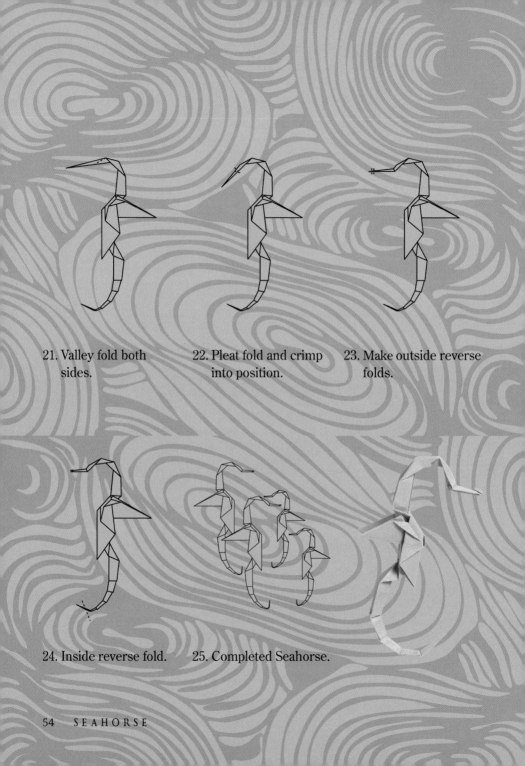

21. Valley fold both sides.

22. Pleat fold and crimp into position.

23. Make outside reverse folds.

24. Inside reverse fold.

25. Completed Seahorse.

FLYING FISH

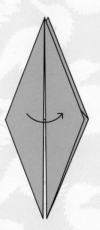

1. Start with Base Fold III. Make valley folds.

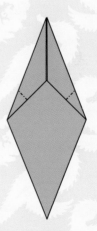

2. Make inside reverse folds.

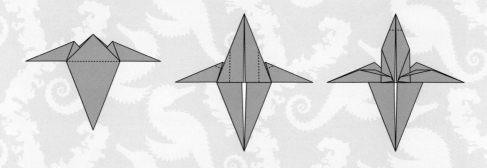

3. Valley fold.

4. Make valley folds.
   Squash at same time.

5. Valley fold.

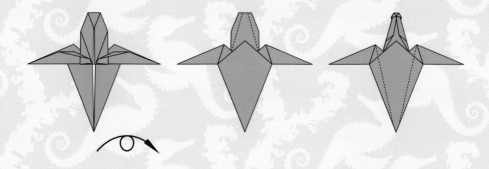

6. Turn over to the other
   side.

7. Make valley folds.

8. Make valley folds.

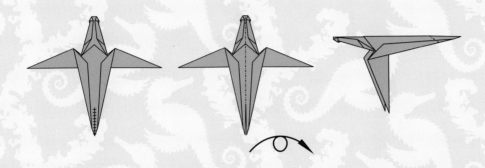

9. Cut as shown.

10. Mountain fold in half, then rotate.

11. Mountain fold.

12. Valley fold.

13. Make valley folds.

14. Open and flatten.

15. Completed Flying Fish.

KILLER WHALE

PART I

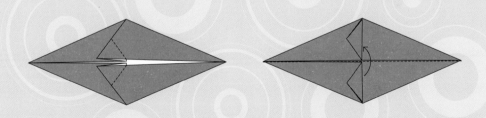

1. Start with Base Fold I, then make valley folds.

2. Valley fold in half.

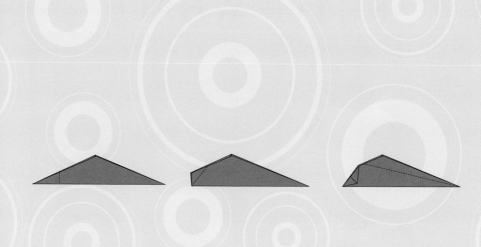

3. Inside reverse fold, as shown.

4. Valley fold front and back.

5. Valley fold front and back.

6. Valley fold front and back for "eyes."

7. Completed part I (top) of Killer Whale.

PART II

1. Start with Base Fold I, then mountain fold in half.

2. Valley fold both sides.

3. Inside reverse fold.

4. Mountain fold front and back.

5. Mountain fold front and back.

6. Completed part II (bottom) of Killer Whale.

TO ATTACH

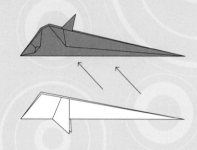

1. Put parts I and II together, as shown, and glue front body part to hold.

2. Cut through layers as indicated; lightly valley fold "tail fin" layers front and back to separate.

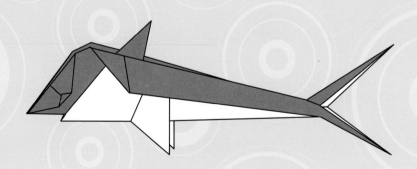

3. Completed Killer Whale.

SWORDFISH

PART I

1. Start with Base Fold I, then mountain fold in half.

2. Valley fold front and back.

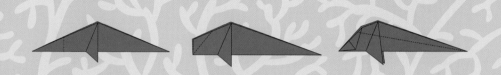

3. Inside reverse fold.

4. Valley fold front and
back.

5. Valley fold front and
back.

6. Make valley folds, for "eyes."

7. Completed part I (rear) of
Swordfish.

PART II

1. Start with Base Fold I,
   then valley fold in half.

2. Make cut through
   layers as indicated.

3. Valley fold each side.

4. Mountain fold inward both front
   and back.

5. Completed part II (front) of
   Swordfish.

TO ATTACH

1. Attach parts I and II together as shown; lightly glue to hold.

2. Make "top fin" cuts to both sides as shown. Lightly inside reverse fold top "tail fin."

3. In the same way, outside reverse fold lower "tail fin." Squash fold both "side fins."

4. Completed Swordfish.

LOBSTER

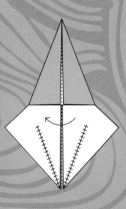

1. Start with Base Fold III. Cut front layer, then unfold.

2. Cut as shown, then valley fold in half.

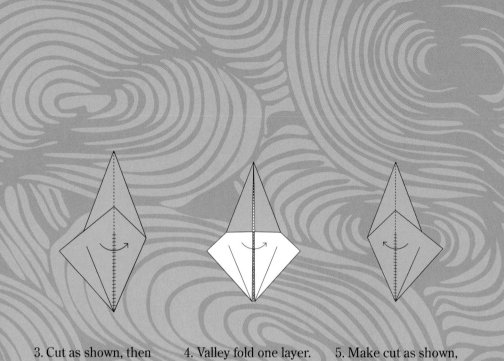

3. Cut as shown, then valley fold back.

4. Valley fold one layer.

5. Make cut as shown, then valley fold back.

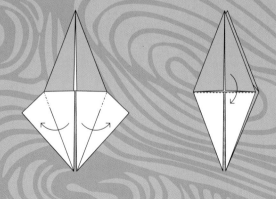

6. Mountain fold flaps to inside.

7. Valley fold.

8. Make inside reverse folds.

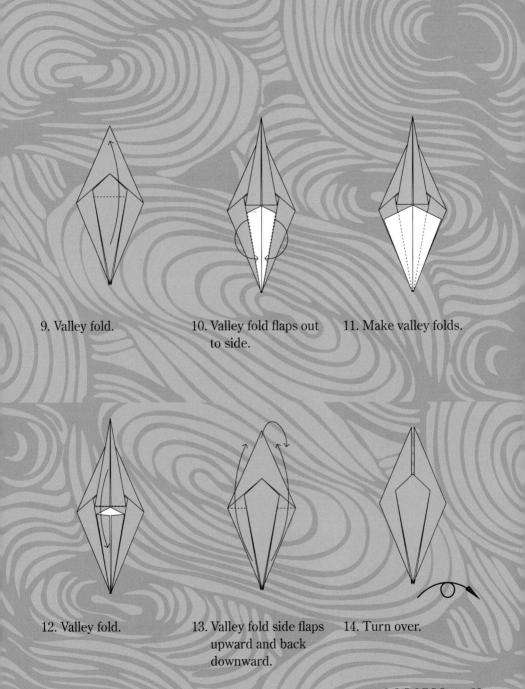

9. Valley fold.

10. Valley fold flaps out to side.

11. Make valley folds.

12. Valley fold.

13. Valley fold side flaps upward and back downward.

14. Turn over.

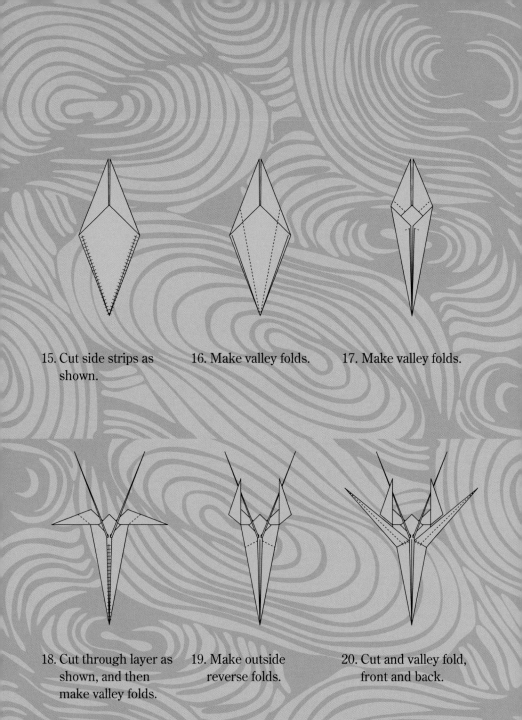

15. Cut side strips as shown.

16. Make valley folds.

17. Make valley folds.

18. Cut through layer as shown, and then make valley folds.

19. Make outside reverse folds.

20. Cut and valley fold, front and back.

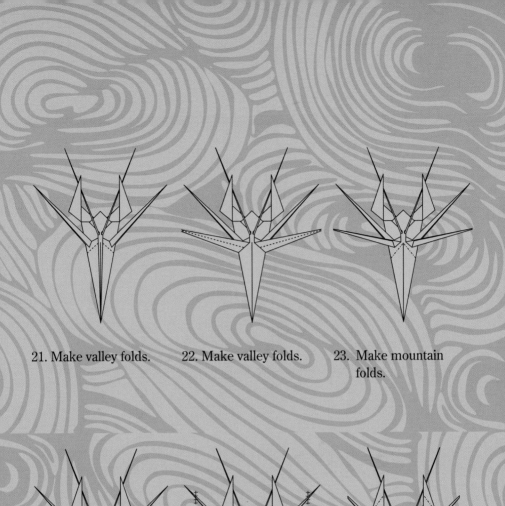

21. Make valley folds.

22. Make valley folds.

23. Make mountain folds.

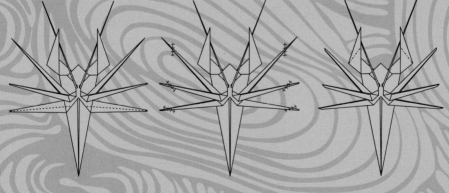

24. Make valley folds.

25. Make cuts as shown.

26. Make inside reverse folds.

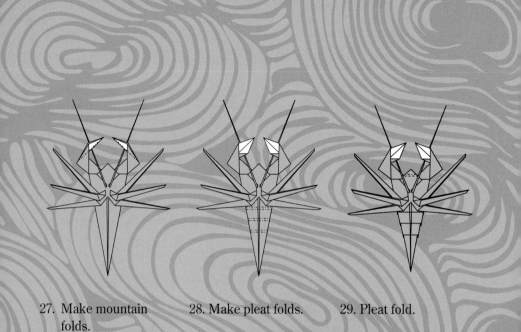

27. Make mountain folds.

28. Make pleat folds.

29. Pleat fold.

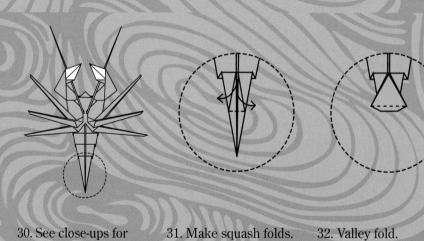

30. See close-ups for detail.

31. Make squash folds.

32. Valley fold.

33. Make cuts as shown.   34. Unfold to sides.   35. Valley fold.

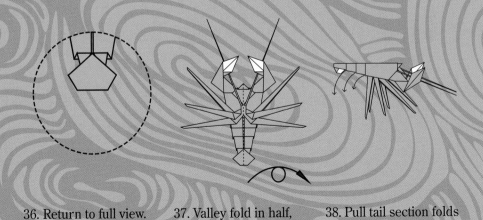

36. Return to full view.   37. Valley fold in half,   38. Pull tail section folds
                                then rotate.   into position as
                                                           shown.

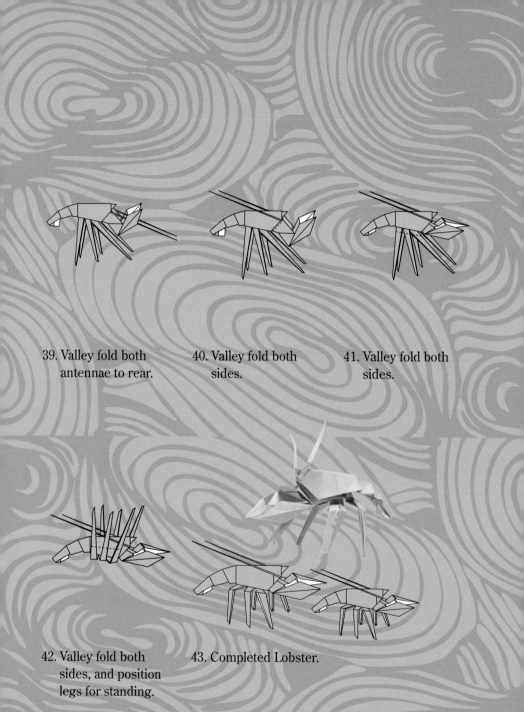

39. Valley fold both antennae to rear.

40. Valley fold both sides.

41. Valley fold both sides.

42. Valley fold both sides, and position legs for standing.

43. Completed Lobster.

TURTLE

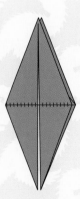

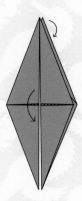

1. Start with Base Fold III. Cut as shown.

2. Valley fold both sides.

3. Make inside reverse folds.

4. Valley fold.

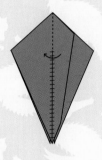

5. Cut and valley fold.

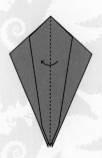

6. Valley fold.

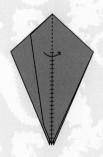

7. Cut and valley fold.

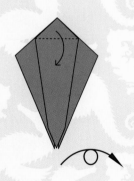

8. Valley fold, and then rotate.

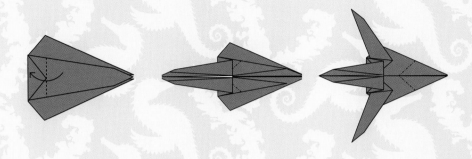

9. Valley fold.

10. Mountain fold.

11. Make mountain folds.

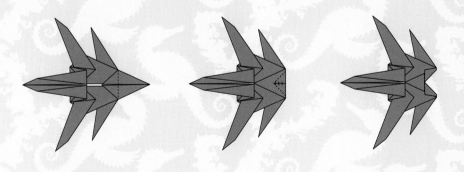

12. Valley fold.

13. Cut and valley fold.

14. Valley fold.

15. Valley fold in half.

16. Pull in direction of arrows, and crimp fold into place.

17. Pleat fold.

18. Pleat fold.

19. Valley fold both sides.

20. Valley fold both sides.

21. Make pleat folds.

22. Inside reverse fold legs.

23. Push down on top to open up body.

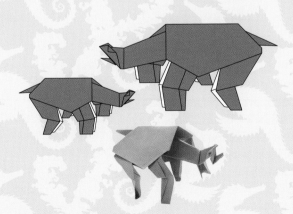

24. Mountain fold all four legs slightly inward.

25. Completed Turtle.

INDEX

Angelfish, 35–38

Coral Fish, 31–34

Dolphin, 26–30

Flying Fish, 55–58

fold lines, 5

folds, base, 12-18

      base fold I, 12

      base fold II, 13

      base fold III, 14–16

      base fold IV, 17–18

folds, basic, 6–11

      inside crimp fold, 11

inside reverse fold, 7

      kite form, 6

      mountain fold, 7

      outside crimp fold, 11

      outside reverse fold, 8

      pleat fold, 9

      pleat fold reverse, 9

      squash fold I, 10

      squash fold II, 10

      valley fold, 6

glue, 4

Hammerhead Shark, 44–49

Horseshoe Crab, 22–25

inside crimp fold, 11

inside reverse fold, 7

instructions, basic, 4

Killer Whale, 59–62

kite form, 6

Lionfish, 39–43

Lobster, 67–74

mountain fold, 7

outside crimp fold, 11

outside reverse fold, 8

paper, origami, 4

pleat fold, 9

pleat fold reverse, 9

Seahorse, 50–54

squaring off paper, 5

squash fold I, 10

squash fold II, 10

Stingray, 19–21

Swordfish, 63–66

symbols & lines, 5

technique, 4

Turtle, 75–79

valley fold, 6

Whale, Killer, 59–62